Akampurira Abraham

Sustainable Development and the Environment

An Aspect of Development

Anchor Compact

Abraham, Akampurira: Sustainable Development and the Environment: An Aspect of Development. Hamburg, Anchor Academic Publishing 2013
Original title of the thesis: Sustainable Development and the Environmen

Buch-ISBN: 978-3-95489-153-5
PDF-eBook-ISBN: 978-3-95489-653-0
Druck/Herstellung: Anchor Academic Publishing, Hamburg, 2013

Bibliografische Information der Deutschen Nationalbibliothek:
Die Deutsche Nationalbibliothek verzeichnet diese Publikation in der Deutschen Nationalbibliografie; detaillierte bibliografische Daten sind im Internet über http://dnb.d-nb.de abrufbar

Bibliographical Information of the German National Library:
The German National Library lists this publication in the German National Bibliography. Detailed bibliographic data can be found at: http://dnb.d-nb.de

All rights reserved. This publication may not be reproduced, stored in a retrieval system or transmitted, in any form or by any means, electronic, mechanical, photocopying, recording or otherwise, without the prior permission of the publishers.

Das Werk einschließlich aller seiner Teile ist urheberrechtlich geschützt. Jede Verwertung außerhalb der Grenzen des Urheberrechtsgesetzes ist ohne Zustimmung des Verlages unzulässig und strafbar. Dies gilt insbesondere für Vervielfältigungen, Übersetzungen, Mikroverfilmungen und die Einspeicherung und Bearbeitung in elektronischen Systemen.

Die Wiedergabe von Gebrauchsnamen, Handelsnamen, Warenbezeichnungen usw. in diesem Werk berechtigt auch ohne besondere Kennzeichnung nicht zu der Annahme, dass solche Namen im Sinne der Warenzeichen- und Markenschutz-Gesetzgebung als frei zu betrachten wären und daher von jedermann benutzt werden dürften.

Die Informationen in diesem Werk wurden mit Sorgfalt erarbeitet. Dennoch können Fehler nicht vollständig ausgeschlossen werden und die Diplomica Verlag GmbH, die Autoren oder Übersetzer übernehmen keine juristische Verantwortung oder irgendeine Haftung für evtl. verbliebene fehlerhafte Angaben und deren Folgen.

Alle Rechte vorbehalten

© Anchor Academic Publishing, ein Imprint der Diplomica® Verlag GmbH
http://www.diplom.de, Hamburg 2013
Printed in Germany

Table of Contents

Chapter one 5
1.1 INTRODUCTION 5
1.2 Purpose of the study. 5
1.3. Definitions. 5
1.4 CONCEPTUAL FRAMEWORK 7

Chapter two 9
2.1 Causes of environmental degradation 9

Chapter three 14
3.0 Impact of environment Mismanagement. 14

Chapter four 21
Environmental Management. 21
4.1 Sustainable agriculture 21
4.2 Mixed Farming. 24
4.3. Multiple cropping 25
4.4. Water management 27
4.5 Management of forest resources. 28
4.6 Improved health for a sustainable development 31
4.7. Environmental management: principles from quantum theory. 33
4.8. Other parameters for sustainable development. 34

Chapter Five. 37
5.0 Recommendations. 37

Chapter six. 44
6.0 Conclusion. 44

Acronyms 46
References 47

Chapter one

1.1 INTRODUCTION.

Man is dependent on the physical environment for his survival. He has however failed to tame it controllably. Man's desire to satisfy his needs have led to increased human use of the environment. Human negligence in addition to collective actions for economic gains has put the environment at a disadvantage.

Many of the natural ecosystems have been interfered with. This has been through encroachment on forest reserves, degradation of wetlands, uncontrollable expansion of agricultural land leading to soil erosion and soil exhaustion, overgrazing and burning of grasslands leading to bear soils that are susceptible to erosion agents. A sustainable situation occurs when man's ability to use natural resources can be replenished naturally. Man's activity has outstretched the ability of these resources to replenish naturally. The interactions of man's current processes with the environment have strained it. The man's disturbance affects the interdependence of the atmosphere, that is, the lithosphere, the hydrosphere and the biosphere which leads to environmental degradation. It has caused negative impact in several ways such as such as global warming, acidification, fossil and resource depletion, photo chemical oxidation, human toxicology, and fresh water aquatic pollution.

1.2 Purpose of the study.

- To aid the people to be aware of the objectives of the principles and perspectives of sustainable development and environmental management.
- To be able to identify the linkages between environment, society and development.
- To develop environmental planning skills.

1.3. Definitions.

Sustainable development is a pattern of resource use, that aims to meet human needs while preserving the environment so that these needs can be met not only in the present but also for generations to come. (United Nations report, 1987). It is very clear that sustainable development involves careful handling of the available resources such that these resources are not extinct for even the future generations to use and enjoy. Since the future generations continue to face the challenge of an increasing population growth rates, the need for more resources for energy and other needs continue to rise. Natural resources should therefore be generously guarded despite intense human activity. This calls for an agreement with the proper resource management so that the future generations can also benefit. Management of resources should be inherent in the people around the world since man is part and parcel of nature. All the people old and young should develop a passion of the environment.

Sustainable development is affected by three major factors for instance environmental, economic and socio-political factors. Therefore to achieve sustainable development, social, economic, and environmental objectives must be met. We cannot sustain development in the long run if we fail to balance social, economic, and environmental objectives. For example to ensure a sustainable development there must be a healthy population that is economically empowered, with a sober mind, educated and with desirable values. Such type of population is as a result of good governance and proper policies.

Globalization provides great opportunities and challenges for sustainable development. Globalization offers opportunities of international trade among nations, investment opportunities, capital flows and technology advancement and transfer for the growth of world economies. This enhances the improvement of people's welfare, a pre requisite to sustainable development. There are still challenges to overcome to meet the desired standards. These include poverty, diseases, political insecurity, unemployment and un equal distribution of incomes among the people in the community. These challenges cause disequilibrium between the growth objectives and sustainable development.

Some of the factors necessary for sustainable development include; proper management of natural resources, poverty eradication, proper cosumption behaviors that results into sustainable production patterns and proper policies in regard to environment management and investment.

1.4 CONCEPTUAL FRAMEWORK

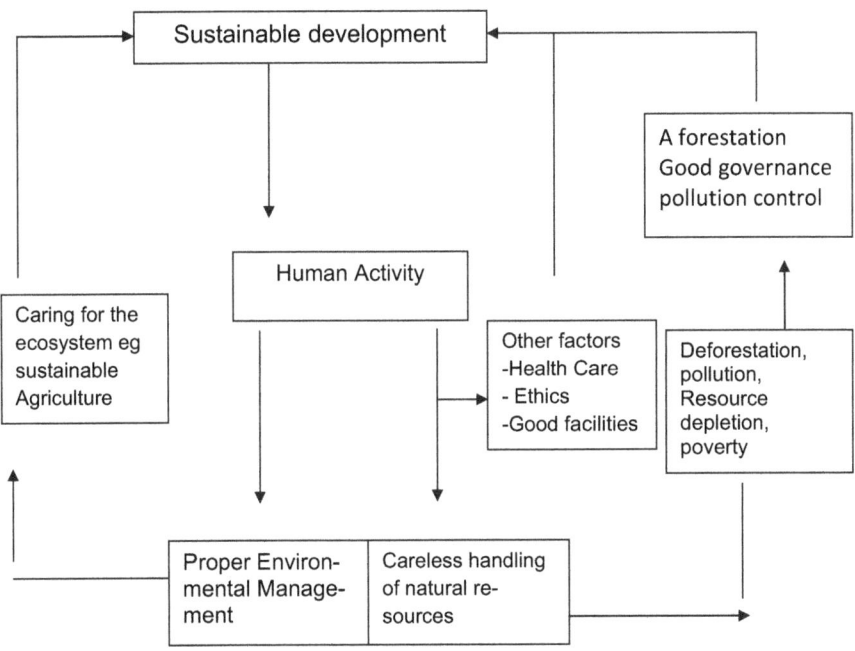

Source: Self developed 2011

Sustainable development and environmental management depends on human activity. When the environment is properly handled in man's endeavor to attain his needs, the ecosystem is maintained thus sustainable development. On the other hand, careless handling of the natural resources through human activity will abuse the environment. The end result will be poverty and hunger, deforestation, pollution, resource depletion and general fall in the welfare of the population. This calls man to revisit his ways of co-existence with the environment without causing any natural conflict. Better methods of dealing with the environment are necessary. These include; a forestation, pollution control, better methods of agriculture that are sustainable. Social economic factors, good governance and policies are also necessary for sustainable development.

Chapter two

2.1 Causes of environmental degradation.

Some of man's activities once not controlled lead to poor management of natural resources. These activities lead to soil erosion, bush enchroachment, deforestation and pollution. These effects generally sum up to environmental degradation. Environmental degradation is a result of mutilateral processes that enchroach on the environment. These include socio-economic, institutional and technological activities on the environment. High agitation for economic growth, intensification of agriculture, rising energy and transportation, and urbanisation results into mismanagement of natural resources thus dynamic environment changes. This is in agreement with NEMA report (2004) which shows that poverty has been and is the major cause of environmental degradation and resuorce depletion. Poverty in the environment fragile areas triggers cause and effect of environmental degradation.

Undesirable land use patterns such as poor farming systems lead to land degradation. These poor farming practices include monocropping, clearing and burning the vegetation and use of rudimentally techniques fo production. Kimaru (2003) points out places that are densely populated such as Kigezi Highlands, vegetative fallowing has been largely abandoned which has resulted into loss of organic matter and soil biodiversity. Soil physical properties and soil nutrients will be affected. Social, economic and technological factors have a big bearing on the farming practices. The cutting of the trees leaves the land bear subjecting it to soil erosion. This leaves the soil layers to be washed to the lowlands. The low lands are subjected to floods that causes loss of lives and property. Common areas which are victims of this include Bududa in Western Uganda.

Deforestation is another cause of environmental degradation. The protective cover of the soil is removed by the need to have more land for agriculture, overgrazing, burning that destroys a vast range of forest land. All this leads to soil erosion, land salination and loss of nutrients from the soil.

The loss of the vegetation cover in the drive to push for industrialisation is becoming unbearable threat to the ecological system.Gastone (2013) explains that environmental disasters such as floods, landslides, drought, hailstorms water scarcity are among the challenges Uganda is going through as the aftereffects of the uncontrolled deforestation. Some of the forested lands is being turned into plantational farms to produce the raw materials for the industries such as Mabira forest Gastone report says. It is evidenced that many parts of forest cover have fallen prey to human economic activity, a situation that is heading most communities to the environmental turmoil.

Photo by Johnan-15th Nov 2011.

The photo was taken in Kitumba, 8 km from Kabale municipality. It depicts the indiscriminate cutting of the trees for charcoal which is on high demand both in Uganda and our neighbouring Rwanda. Charcoal burning has created an environmental disaster in Kabale district and many other parts in the country side. The end result has always been excessive soil erosion on the hillsides and floods in the lowlands leading to loss of property and lives. Another example is from Central America which registered a decline in forest cover by 19% between 1990-2005. This loss of the vegetation cover was primarily by expansion of agriculture and cattle ranching.

A high rate of increased population directly impacts on the environment. A high rate of population growth increase pressure on the availabe resources and results in environmental stresses like loss of biodiversity, air and water pollution and increased pressure on arable land. There is also the dependency burden that affects the individuals of the working population. A lot is spent on the big families and so little is saved for investiment. This eventually lead to the persistent viscous cycle of poverty.

Rural urban migration that comes as a result of failure to have jobs from which to earn some income in rural areas. People move to urban centres to look for jobs. This has rapidly increased population numbers in the urban areas. This therefore exerts a lot of pressure on the available resources such as housing, energy, education, health, transport water, and recreational ammenities. It leads to the deteriorating of social services such as water and air , growth of slums and congestion.

Transport activities is one of the causes of environmental degradation. This is in form of air pollution, noise and oil spills from marine shipping. In Uganda a lot of very old vehicles are seen on the road causing pollution to the atmosphere. There is no time limit for which a vehicle should be used on the road. Some vihicles are in poor mechanical condition causing a lot of pollution to the atmosphere. They are also a threat to human life since they are among the major causes of road accidents.

Rapid expansion of the cities that is at times un planned results into degradation of urban. A lot of crime is also observed in many cities that involve theft and robbery. The rapid expansion widens the gap between supply and demand for services like energy, education, water, and recreational services. This has subsequently led to congestion and pollution. This is common in almost all cities of the world including those of the developed world. Pennington, David W, Versmann, Andreas. (2011) talk about the amount of waste generated in Europe and beyond, by the production and consumption patterns of the masses. They add to say that a proper waste management is essential in order to reduce detrimental environmental impacts. A high sense of waste management need to be planted in the population. Uganda and Rwanda are two neighboring countries with different cultures as far as waste management is concerned. In Uganda people deposit waste any how whereas the Rwandese are very careful in waste management. This is due to the strictness of the law in Rwanda. In Uganda the people do not respect the law due to rising corruption, lack of roll models among other factor among other factors

The manufacturing technology has caused harm to the environment. This is evidenced by intensive resource and energy use causing resource depletion, water, air and pollution and degradation of the ecosystem. There are huge amounts of industrial and hazardous wastes that cause serious environmental health problems. As far as industrialization is concerned, there is a lot of wasted waste. There is waste and misuse of the environment as well as increased environmental degradation. There is an increased moral degeneration to the workers in the industry and this affects sustainable development. Secondary, industrialists aim at profit maximization at the expense of the welfare of the community. Externalities lead to the deterioration of the living standards of the people.

Some countries do not respond to environmental strategies because of their persistent debt burdens. Such countries overexploit the earth's resources to get cash to cover the debts. They deliberately cut on social, health, environmental conservation and other important programs for community welfare with the aim of coming out of the huge debt. For example, Honduras and Nicaragua, where Hurricane Mitch devastated large parts of these countries as well as Mozambique and Madagascar where floods have made hundreds of thousands of people homeless. It is important to tackle debt problems for such countries so as to easily attain environmental targets.

The effect of consumerism has been observed to be one of the key problems towards environmental management around the world. Consumption patterns have changed a great deal. There is overconsumption that strains the available resources. Such mass consumption calls for the matching supply to make the situation in equilibrium. The level mass consumption has been rapidly growing and has had an impact on the environment. How do we consume and for what purposes determines how we extract resources. This creates the type of products needed on the market that ends up with pollution and waste. It therefore directly affects environmental degradation, poverty, hunger and also obesity that is on the rise. Solutions to the problems like poverty, hunger, environmental degradation and other related problems need to be sought by researchers, policy makers in consultation with the local communities.

Poor disposal of polythene bags is also detrimental to the environment. The polythene bags once poorly disposed choke the environment because they do not decay. Atuheire (2012) explains that it is important to replace the unfriendly environment polythene bags with those made out of banana fibres. She adds that products such as paper, carpets, and fabrics can be made out of banana fibres.

Chapter three

3.0 Impact of environment Mismanagement.

As more and more people move from rural to urban areas, the carrying capacity of the roads, railways, hospitals, schools telecommunications services accommodation and transport services is outstretched. This high demand for infrastructure requires public and private cooperation. The rate of urbanization is increasing due to the shift of people from rural to urban areas. Cities are experiencing an increasing strain on their existing infrastructural systems for instance on power grids, roadways, telecommunication lines, accommodation and transport services.

For example using a flexible grid infrastructure in the North-East US in 2003 to meet the demand for power. These back outs can be over come by having an environmentally friendly and affordable energy grid system to match the energy demand. In Uganda most of the energy sources are not tapped; such as wind, solar, and bio gas. The country depends on hydro electric power, fire wood and charcoal for its energy needs and this greatly strains these energy sources. Rural electrification is still poor and therefore the rural basically depends on wood for their energy hence a major cause for environmental degradation. NEMA Report (1998) points out that, in rural areas where land gets degraded, livelihoods are threatened in form of decline in food, increased famine and loss of income and consequently, reduction in the access to any goods and services attached to them.

Lakes have been polluted by human activities. This water is meant for human and animal use. For example L. Bunyonyi water is used for domestic and industrial use in Kabale town, whereas L. Victoria is a source of water for Kampala, Jinja and Masaka. Communities around the lakes are sensitized to plant trees and reduce activities that pollute these lakes. Not only do trees improve on the quality of air we breath, they also purify the water that goes into the lakes. Bian, Bo, Cheng, Xiao-Juano; Li, Lei (2011) explain that Road deposited sediments (RDS) is an important environmental medium for impacting the characteristics of pollutants in storm water run-off; it is of critical importance to investigate the water quality of urban environments. Urban water quality in urban cities is poor due a lot of human activity. The urban environment is stretched by a high population pressure. In some of the cities, there is lack of enough toilets and city dwellers tend to dispose the waste poorly that ends up contaminating water and the air. It ultimately leads to poor health of the population. There is still outbreak of dysentery, cholera and typhoid that is reported in some urban canters. Investigation of water quality is therefore very important for the health of the people.

It is believed that Uganda is prone to diseases such as Marburg and Ebola because of tampering with the wildlife. Agatha (2012) puts it that Ebola and Marburg hemorrhagic fever occurs in places near forests that have been encroached on by the human activity such as cutting trees, leaving the place open for wildlife to interface with man. Dr. Lwamafa (2012) explains that where optimal conditions exist for direct interface of man and wildlife, there will be transmission of diseases which are not typically human diseases, moving from wild animal kingdom to human beings through the environment. Ebola and Marburg have been a threat in some parts of Uganda and these are contagious diseases whose chances to survive are minimal.

The negative consequences of rapid urban population growth and industrialization greatly affect the environment. This is as a result of increased demand for charcoal and food. This therefore will affect the vegetation cover for charcoal burners and food producers who clear land in search of more agricultural land. However the rapid population growth generates demand that encourages industrialization.

According to media reports, Musamya river is heavily polluted by industrial waste from the sugar cooperation of Uganda limited. The water quality of this river is poor due to untreated waste released from the industry. Fish and animals die which shows that the water is poisonous. The residents complain that they develop skin rashes when they swim or bathe in that river. The resident James Wakabu of Wasswa village complains "We have been rendered helpless because we are very poor. The resource that we used to enjoy freely has been taken away". The other problem noted on the river is its bad smell. A tourist guide at Griffin campsite, complains that because of the smelly water, tourists do not enjoy the local dishes which used be a source of revenue to the people in that village. Apart from the pollution, consultants discovered that the river is too silted to sustain life reports say. Even before waste is released from the industry into river Musamya, the color of the water is brown. This is as a result of siltation due to rampant cutting down of trees and destruction of wetlands in the river's catchment.

One of the fresh bodies is L. Wamala in central Uganda. It is associated with several rivers and wetlands including river Katonga that drains into L. Victoria. Lake Wamala is of historical, ecological, economic and socio-cultural significance. Unfortunately, its size has shrunk due to half its original size during the 1990's (UNEP, 2009). In addition to human induced activities, climate variability is reported to be a cause if this. For example, UNEP (2009) reported that this shallow lake's levels have fluctuated with changes in precipitation through the recent decades. All this is a result of tampering with the natural systems by human activity that has caused environmental changes. A fluctuation in the water level affects the growth of the aquatic organisms and a pull back to the ecosystem.

Poor agricultural practices are commonly practiced in many parts of the world. These make the soil to get depleted. Burning is done to clear the fields that destroy the flora and fauna. This distorts the ecosystem. The plants that provide the habitat for animals and birds are destroyed. Some of the hills in Kigezi which used to be bushy in the 1980's are now bare and therefore subject to constant soil erosion. When we were growing up, we used to see geese, mongooses and monkeys. They are not seen now days because of forest destruction in these areas. Also many tree species that used to work as medicinal trees are almost extinct.

High population pressure has led to wide exploitation of the forest cover. For example, at the beginning of the 20th century, Uganda's tropical high forests covered 3,090,000 ha or 12% of the country's area. Over the years, the forests have been gradually cleared and today estimates indicate reduction to about 730,000 ha which is only 3% of Uganda's area (NEMA).

Burning is a bad habit that is used by pastoralists to burn old grass during the dry season so that fresh grass can sprout during the rainy season. This is done in hilly areas of Kabale, Kanungu, Kisoro and Rukungiri in the western Uganda. In these areas can destroy vegetation up to a 10 km radius. All these are poor management practices. Burning also applies to swamps by the hunters in Rushebeya and Buriime in Kabale district.

Timber extraction for commercial purposes is one of the major causes of forest degradation. It results into various hectares of tree cover exposing the soil to agents of erosion such as water and wind. Deforestation contributes to global warming. It is reported that tropical deforestation is responsible for approximately 20% of the world green house gas emissions. During the process of photosynthesis, trees and other vegetation plants remove carbon dioxide from the atmosphere and then release oxygen back to the atmosphere during normal respiration. Since forests are able to extract carbon dioxide and other pollutants from the atmosphere, it leads to the stability of the biosphere. There is no vegetation to balance the gas exchange in the atmosphere once the trees and forests are cleared. Degradation of vegetation leads to loss of forest cover and this creates negative effects because of the influence on carbon exchange. There will be no trees and forests to purify the air. Trees are meant to absorb the excess carbon dioxide from the atmosphere. There is high capacity of vegetation to store huge amounts of carbon for example an average of 30 tonnes of carbon per hectare, decreases when vegetation is depleted. It is noted that soils in the dry zones store a substantial amount of carbon. Soil conservation is important because it regulates carbon in the carbon cycle.

Secondary, the water cycle is affected by deforestation. Plants use their roots to extract water from the soil and release it to the atmosphere through a process of evaporation. After deforestation, little moisture is released to the atmosphere leading to dry climatic conditions. This affects the precipitation levels and reduced water levels in lakes and rivers. For example R. Nile in Uganda has always faced water volume fluctuations that normally affect L. Victoria volumes.

Poverty is one of the factors that have worsened environmental degradation. It is reported that almost half of the population of the world, (about 3 billion people) live on less than $2.50 a day. The poor population derives their survival from the environment. In Uganda, agriculture is a predominant activity in rural areas. This agricultural practice is done on a small scale to produce unmanufactured exports abroad. The economy is heavily dependent on agricultural products that are the main source of foreign exchange. Prices of these products always fluctuate and are dependant on global factor variations. This causes limited supply in the world market and thus little incomes. A negotiation for debt relief due to consistent fall in export earnings is inevitable. Agriculture employs more than 80% of the Uganda's population and this makes the rural economy and not the urban economy the most important in terms of national wealth, household welfare and employment creation. Unfortunately production is on small scale that cannot guarantee a major force to pull the majority of the population out of poverty.

Households in the rural economy operate small economies. They entirely depend on their family labor to do household work and agricultural production. They use rudiment ally tools such as hoes to till the land, and axes to clear the land and baskets to reap the harvest. Less than 9% of the population has regular access to electricity, and more than 90% of Uganda's total energy is provided for using charcoal and firewood. The majority are involved in small agricultural practices and small businesses in the informal sector as a means of survival. However this sector employs the majority of the Ugandans. This is far below the ordinary standard to grant for sustainable development.

The challenge of poverty alleviation has been on top of the agenda of most developing countries. It however meets a hurdle of environmental destruction as the population intensifies on major human activities such as agriculture to earn incomes. The 60% of the world population who are found in susceptible areas are in remote and ecologically vulnerable areas. In these areas it is a big challenge to implement poverty alleviation programs due to economic, social and cultural factors. An example of the communities of Batwa in Kabale, and the Bakonjo in the

Rwenzori mountains in Kasese district is cited. It has been estimated that 80% of the poor people in Latin America live in such areas, 60% in Africa and 50% in Asia. In a bid to attain growth in some economies, it has imposed severe implications not only to the poor people but also for the environment. It has always become very difficult for residents in theses areas to abandon them for other sectors of the economy as was the case in Europe in the last century, are not promising. They are contented in their ways of life and do not recognize the essence of changing to another way of living and operation. It has resulted into rapid degradation and poverty crusts of these areas.

It is important to note these features in the fragile ecosystems;

(a) Most of the world resources are found in the susceptible areas. For example 40% of the earth's land surface is regarded dry land. Out of this, 70% is already degraded or subject to heavy degradation. These areas are sources of water, agricultural products, minerals, and a home for endangered species for example Bwindi impenetrable forest that is a home for mountain gorillas.

(b) The importance of ecosystems can be emphasized in especially in terms of human habitat. For example approximately 900 million of the world's population is deriving their livelihood in these areas. This is a clear indication that they are greatly affected by environment changes. It is noted that although only about 10% of the world population live in mountainous areas, approximately 40% occupies the watersheds below these mountains. The mountain ecosystem therefore directly affects the life of the half of the world's population. An example is from the Andes to Himalayas' and from the South East Asia to East and Central Africa. The story is exactly the same for the Eastern parts and Western Uganda where there is a dense population on the foot of the mountains. In such areas, the ecosystem is highly tampered with through by man's activity. For example deforestation and strive to attain economic growth. This calls for countries and the international community to come to rescue these disadvantaged people in susceptible areas.

There are poor services like schools, health care and road net work thus persistent poverty.

(c) Approximately 300 million of the absolute poor in ecological susceptible areas are indigenous peoples. They derive their livelihood on natural resources. This has caused to the livelihood adaptation to the harsh conditions in which they live. It is important for resource conservation in the areas to be built upon indigenous knowledge. This is because methods and traditional knowledge of the natural resources and environment constitutes a rich human heritage. Sustainable measures to fight poverty and conserve the environment are easily generated using the community.

(d) Rural women are the most affected by the environment change. They are the key players in agriculture, home activities such as collection of firewood, water and food for their families. This makes women to be more vulnerable than men to the effects environmental degradation. Poverty in the home also affects women more than men since they take care of education, health, food, fuel and energy requirements of the family. Women are poorly represented at local and national level and therefore have continued to be victims of environment change and have least benefited on poverty alleviation programs.

Chapter four

Environmental Management.

Environmental management through research offers technologies on use and conservation of natural resources, protection of habitats and control of environmental damage. It is a practice that reconciles the conflict between human rising needs and the protection of natural resources. The natural environment is very supportive and therefore important to man. It provides services that include raw materials, water management, erosion control, carbon storage, climate regulation, and nutrient cycling among others. Environmental management will be achieved through the following ways:

4.1 Sustainable agriculture.

This is an environment friendly method of agriculture that allows the production of crops or livestock without the damaging the environment. Sustainable agriculture avoids the negative effects on the land resources and general biodiversity disturbance for instance water, soil, vegetation and animal life. It aims at improved and conserved natural science than aiming at pollution or depletion. Under sustainable agriculture, better farming practices are done and in this case animals and crops are raised together for maximum benefit and sustainable management. There is mutual relationship between what human activity intends to derive in agro forestry. Under this practice, maximum benefit will lead to improved living conditions of the people and a well managed ecosystem.

A case in point is cited in Cuba. When Cuba faced a crisis of survival when it lost its capacity to import some goods like petroleum, fertilizers, agricultural machinery and other production inputs, the country undertook a structural reorganization within the agricultural sector. This involved the agri-ecological production of food for consumption in and around cities. Koont (2011: 1) asserts that the government's ultimate goal was to make Cuba self sufficient in meeting the nutritional needs of the population through small scale agriculture reliant on human labor rather than machinery and chemicals. This is important in achieving sustainable development in the following ways;

i. Minimizes unemployment since the majority of the populations are involved in the various agricultural activities.
ii. It makes production of organic food products possible since the grass root people cannot afford expensive technologies and other chemical inputs especially in the developing world.
iii. It gives an opportunity families to be self reliant in food production which guarantees food security to communities..
iv. Improving the nutritional needs of the population is made possible and this helps to eradicate nutritional deficiency diseases that affect the growth of infants in most communities of the world.
v. The local population can easily adapt to the local climatic and demand conditions.

Cuba has registered a significant success in having a balanced food basket through raising livestock for protein and fruit and vegetable growing that provide vitamins among the population.

Umrani etal (2010: 17) emphasizes that farming sustainability means growing crops and livestock in the ways that simultaneously meet three objectives;

- Economic profit. This helps households to attain their basic needs such as medical care, housing, clothing for their welfare
- Social benefits to the family and the community which helps to allow a better environment in which people relate and support with each other.
- Environmental conservation which helps to preserve all animal and plant species for a friendly and sustainable ecological system.

Proper agricultural development aids in environmental conservation as well as boosting income generation. Millennium Promise (2011) reports that further progress in income generation requires continued investments in agriculture for instance in form of irrigation, to enable multi-season cropping cropping and cultivation of high value crops.

4.2 Mixed Farming.

Many farmers in the world over, practice agriculture of having crops and animals raised on the same plot. Under this practice interdependence of plants and animals takes place for example plants provide food to the animals whereas animals supply manure to the plants. In places like Kigezi region where shortage of food is attributed to soils losing fertility each family is urged to keep at least a heifer or some cows and sheep to provide manure to the depleted soils. This is meant to restore food security in families. The farmer is able to diversify production of crops on the same plot of land. It will caterer for food security in societies. It allows the farmer to use labor effectively. The same unit of labor will look after the different enterprises on the farm. Mixed farming leads to sustainable development since land and other resources are optimally utilized. The environment is friendly treated to provide man's food. Crops benefit from plants and plants also benefit the animals causing a harmonious ecosystem. No party deprives others from living in the ecosystem.

In the fishing sector, there is uncontrolled fishing in some communities and this puts the fish species at stake. Namutebi (2012), notes that some factories manufacturing the fish nets do not mind about the net sizes. The fish nets that are manufactured are under size which poses the danger of the fish stock being depleted.

4.3. Multiple cropping

Multiple cropping involves planting of more than one crop on the same piece of land. It may include annual crops being planted with perennials or annual crops planted together for the sake of maximizing output among other importance. This practice maximizes the field by the farmer hence more food and cash.

When the farmer grows many different crops, disease and pest out break is controlled. Loss is therefore avoided. The practice avoids Insects and pests are attracted by the monoculture system.

Tree crops and annual vegetable crops can be inter-planted in strips on contour to prevent erosion. Legume trees planted in between the rows will fix nitrogen into the soil that is important for plant growth. There is soil fertility rejuvenation and maximum yield from the piece of land. More cash will therefore be realized. Crop rotation is also important for preserving soil fertility and thus ensuring better crop growth that is essential for food security.

Multiple cropping when adopted lead to sustainable management of natural resources. It is a farming practice that involves planting two or more crops together on the same unit of land. There is maximum utilization of each unit of labor and land employed and other resources to obtain maximum possible yield. Multiple cropping can also be done on a rotational basis to ensure that there is adequate nitrogen fixed to the soil and other related advantages like improving soil structure when deep rooted crops alternate with shallow rooted crops on the same piece of land.

Low Carbon Development (LCD) has become an international concern for the improved environment management. It has become a hot issue on international forums. It involves low carbon growth for the sake of a safe environment. There is however limited experience and knowledge of appropriate incentives, costs, benefits and available funding.

Carbon Plus is one of the international programs meant to develop emergent forest carbon. It helps to prevent deforestation (REDD+), improved forest management (IFM), and reforestation. In East Africa, this program has not yet taken root. The population in the region has not yet understood how it operates. However efforts are under way to develop this program that is meant to save the environment. Some pilot projects are already being implemented in this region. It is important for governments in this region to disseminate information about carbon rights to the entire population. The concept of carbon rights is still new in these countries (Uganda, Kenya and Tanzania). It is important to note that non of these countries has yet developed a policy and legal framework that incorporates carbon rights. This leaves the population un aware of these carbon rights and this does not help the project implementers to achieve the intended objective of achieving deforestation prevention, improved forest management and reforestation in these countries.

In Bushenyi District (Uganda), a project that examines the benefit sharing arrangements under Trees for Global Benefit Initiative is being implemented. It has been designed as a cooperative, community based carbon offset scheme that puts emphasis on saving the environment through proper and improved land use practices. Participants undertake project activities in return for a payment for ecosystem services (PES) that acts as an incentive for resource conservation. Participants receive staged payments for carrying out activities that generate ecosystem services, measured in tones of carbon. According to NEMA, Mabira forest reserve captures about 17.1 million tones of CO_2, Saving Uganda $bn 1.4 in annual cleaning costs.

4.4. Water management.

Water is a universal necessity for life. Increasingly polluted and diminishing fresh water supplies threaten health and food security and affects economic growth. In Central America, only 21% of the fresh water available in 1950 remains today. This trend is due to extensive deforestation and lack of incentives for sustainable land use.

Dry beds have resulted as a result of poor water management system. Climate change due to long droughts is one of the major contributors of river dry beds. The environment management is very important to keep a stable climate. Drying of the river beds leaves some invertebrates to suffer leading to their extinction. Steward, Alisha L, (2011), explains that dry river beds are physically harsh and they often differ substantially in substrate, topography, and microclimate and inundation frequency from adjacent riparian zones. Given these differences, dry river beds provide a unique habitat for terrestrial invertebrates. The dry beds form a habitat of other animal and plant species, but the original species in the habitat mostly face extinction.

Provision of the upper catchments above villages and valleys help to prevent soil erosion; rebuild eco-systems and slow water across landscape. Forests restore the water table making the river to flow throughout the year. Richard Kimbowa (2013) asked the government to expedite the implementation of the EAC policy on climate change. Experts have warned some water resources such as around L.victoria which is believed to have faced enormous ecological changes. These changes are related to problems of poverty, high population growth rate, land degradation, water quality and declining agricultural productivity. It is very important to avoid washing in streams and rivers as soap and detergents pollute the water for downstream users. This also applies to cleaning vehicles and disposal of industrial waste.

Another notable challenge in the urban areas is where waste disposal pollutes the environment. This is observed in towns and other urban centers like Kabale and

Kampala. Poor waste disposal by the city residents turn out to become a healthy hazard. It poses threat to the growing population. Recycling waste is one of the strategies that should be adopted to reduce waste in urban centers. This can be achieved through commitment of urban authorities. The informal sector, community based organizations, non-governmental organizations and the private sector should be involved in policy and implementation of sustainable sewage management programs. Sanneh, E.S (2011) explains that resource recovery, not waste disposal must be the ultimate goal with clearly defined end user markets so that the recovery loop is complete. He continues to say that sorting of waste at household level would help greatly in making recycling activity successful. It is important to note that in many cases, waste becomes a problem to the population in urban centers, yet this waste is a resource. It only needs to be cycled. As Sanneh asserts, sorting of waste should be done at household level to avoid unnecessary contamination and pollution. A clearly sort waste of materials reduces wastage of this waste matter. Waste is composed of glass, polythene in some cases, and decomposing materials. All these should be sorted at earlier stages for easy recycling process. This form of arrangements reduces on land and water pollution. Employment is also created by the emerging industries related to garbage and waste collection and recycling.

4.5 Management of forest resources.

Use of Fuel Efficient Burning stoves. As shown in figure (b), it saves fossil fuel and eventually lead to sparing use of forest resources. At school, the head cook, Geiger prepares food for 1250 students. The energy saving stove has reduced the amount of firewood by 50%. In the past he would use two Lorries of firewood to prepare for the same number of students in one week. It has therefore saved on the school finances. One lorry of firewood costs Ug. sh.200,000 which totals to approximately Ug sh. 800,000 in one month.

Fig a   Fig. b

The old stove needed a lot of firewood to heat up. There was a lot of energy loss to the environment instead of heating up the heating utensil. This is reflected in figure a.

It would take long to make food ready on top of wasting a lot of firewood. The energy saving stove constructed in figure (b) minimizes energy loss. There is little smoke and food prepared is safer for human consumption. The new technology employs people who earn a living out of the innovative ideas on top of saving the environment. These stoves have also been introduced in the villages by government through NEMA (National Environmental Management Authority). Community members engaged in forest and water stewardship activities receive priority when stoves are introduced to a village. In exchange for receiving a stove, each family commits to either protection or reforestation of nearby forests or adopting agro forestry, which trees to the landscape.

The sustainability of forested ecosystems needs a lot of attention. It often requires cross-boundary management at large spatial scales. It has been noted that this can be challenging. This is with cases where forests are primarily under small scale and or private ownership. This has caused world private forest management to be regulated by government. It is meant to promote more consistent cross-boundary outcomes and better protection of large scale economic integrity. In this qualitative, grounded theory' study, 109 stakeholders throughout the state of Washington, USA were interviewed to learn their perspectives about processes and effects of private forest regulation. Washington has had a well established and comprehensive policy on forest regulatory policies that has provided an excellent study area for this topic. In the study, interviewees included private forest owners, forest policy advisors, regulatory agency employees, and representatives from forest ownership organizations, forest trade groups, and environmental organizations. It is reported that the study revealed an important and often poorly recognized outcome of private forest regulatory policy: regulation rarely affects all private forest owners similarly. Instead the burdens and advantages of regulation tend to be unevenly distributed within this key stakeholder group. The study identified three phenomena producing these inequitable incomes. These include; natural landscape variability, oversights in policy design, and goals among the forest owners.

I would like to apply this study to some extent to the resource management in Uganda. The private sector has not had an opportunity to own forests reserves as per say. Forest reserves are majorly owned by government. These include Mabira, Mafuga Imaramagambo, Bwindi Impenetrable and very many others. However the community has a big stake on these forests. The forest regulation policy has been interfered with by politics. Good policies on forest management have not been properly implemented because of fear to loose in elections by either the presidents or the legislatures. Good policies have always ended up not being implemented. This is observed by what the aspirants propose when they are seeking for votes when they are going to parliament and local councils and what they say after they have attained these seats. They seem to be good policy makers but fear to lose their seats in the coming elections. For example, in the struggle to liberate wetlands, National Environment Management Authority

Ariho (2013) however says that there is deliberate effort to control soil erosion on the highlands of Kabale where Hot- Consult in partnership with the community are planting medicinal trees, digging trenches, and promoting terrace bands. This program once properly implemented will bail out the natural resources from being depleted.

(NEMA) failed to implement policy on wetland encroachment in areas of Kampala city, Kabale; forest encroachment in Kibale, Hoima, Kamwenge and so on. There was interference of politicians from these areas that fear to be unseated in the coming elections when the policy affects their electorates.

Secondary another problem emanates from politicians' lack of will and passion for the forest. A case in point is the recent give-away of Mabira to investor's sugar cane growing even when there is a vast range of unused land in central Uganda. This does not make regulatory laws work properly. Politicians tend to ignore the advice from experts and researchers. These leaders have not become good stewards of our local resources.

4.6 Improved health for a sustainable development

It is necessary to keep the populations physically healthy through primary health care. This is through immunization programs, nutrition workshops and capacity building in societies. It will empower the population economically, a health population that is able to undergo production so as to explore the micro economic opportunities to come out of poverty. With a healthy and educated population, maximum production is expected for an increased economic growth. HIV and AIDS have affected most communities where the sick suffer from stigma and incur a lot of expenses in treatment. Some NGO's such as TASO (The AIDS Support Organization) have tried to help the infected and the affected but a lot needs to be done. Some patients do not access the drugs which normally lead to death and many are subsequently orphaned, a situation that perpetuates dependency burden. There is need to educate communities about the realities of HIV/AIDS. There is also need to offer economic opportunity that will enable the affected to have economic empowerment. Healthy choices for the body, mind and soul where the population should be encouraged on healthy eating habits such as feeding on fruits and vegetables as well as physical body exercises. Dora Byamukama (2013) asserts that social structures should be encouraged to ensure physical security and social support.

Economic sustainability: Agenda 21 clearly identified information, integration and participation as key building blocks to help countries achieve development that recognizes these important pillars. Its emphasis should be highly recognized. Sustainable development can be achieved if countries actively participate in trade and use all the available information to explore growth opportunities. Countries must change from traditional ways of doing business to modern approaches to gain from trade and international cooperation. In the adopted modern methods, integration of environmental issues should be part of development agenda for all countries. This is a holistic development process that does not ignore issues that affect the population at the expense of economic growth. When all population concerns are put into consideration, sustainable development will be achieved.

This is information age where everyone an important agent in information provision and use. A sustainable system does not ignore any part in regard to information provision and information usage. For the case of the environment, it is both the researchers and the rural communities that are well versed with the conditions that they are in touch with. The researcher in the field has to be in touch with the affected in order to get useful information. Policy implementation is easier when the grass root population is involved in the prior planning.

Environmental sustainability keeps the water cycle in harmony with other natural systems that affect animals and plants. Environmental sustainability makes sure that man's activity to use natural resources does not go beyond their carrying capacity. Resources are well managed and the natural environment is replenished naturally. The sustainable management or resources is based on three types of capital; economic, social and natural capital. Natural capital comprises of nature's total resources.

These resources may be non-substitutable and their consumption may be irreversible. They can be regarded as consumables since at times they cannot be replaced. Daly (1991) for example, points to the fact that natural capital can not necessarily be substituted by economic capital. Some resources can be replaced even though it is very clear that some natural ecosystems such as the protection of the ozone layer cannot be replaced. It is important to note that the natural, social, and economic capital complement each other. Their complimentarily role plays a big part in sustained environment and development. There is also substitutability attached to the three types of capital. One of the obstacles of substitutability obstacle to lies in the multiple roles that natural resources serve. For example forests on top of providing for fossil energy, they provide paper, maintain the biodiversity, absorb carbon dioxide and regulate water flow. Paper provision can be substituted by use of wheat and sugarcane hence many sources of paper raw materials.

4.7. Environmental management: principles from quantum theory.

Management of the environment is for any health care provider. Turmoil, multiple relationships and the new ways of "doing business" characterize today's health care system, and traditional management techniques, based on Newtonian physics may no longer be effective. Principles helpful for managing the current health care environment may be found in quantum theory. These include (1) the world is unpredictable (2) the extent of the observer influences how the world is seen (3) interrelations are what count, not the things themselves. These principles are derived from the work of Wheatley, who applied the quantum theoretical framework to leadership. Strategies for gaining competence in managing the new environment are explored. Such strategies include shared governance, the process of delegation, and coordination of services. These strategies may be helpful to colleagues in education as well as in practice.

This theory is important for the preservation of natural resources. The human beings not easily identify with the environment. They see themselves as masters of the environment. Unfortunately there is little passion for the environment that is inherent. During the open day we had at school last month, I asked more than twenty students about what they treasure most on this earth. The feedback I got was that these students do not identify themselves with the environment. They are interested in becoming rich. On the side of professionalism, about only 10 % would like to be environmentalists. This is for the purpose of earning a living. There is no passion developed for the environment.

Secondary, when you follow what people talk about, their conversations are full of commerce, social issues, and how to survive in this world. They rarely talk about the environment. Their relation with the environment is neglected.

4.8. Other parameters for sustainable development.

Shared governance is paramount towards environment as Wheatley says. Shared responsibility in managing resources is key for their sustenance. The community, civil service, the private sector and the institutions has a role to do in preserving the environment. Ignoring any of the concerned parties will not yield the desired results.

There is need to develop a bond between the environment and the human being because interrelations are very important. This can be done through massive education programs about the environment, making people understand that environmental management is the key to sustainable development.

There is a big relationship between poverty and the state of environment as has been recognized by the international community. It is also noted that the environment quality is a key factor of achieving sustainable development. It is therefore achieving quality environment before dreaming sustainable development. For example goal number seven of the millennium Development Goals (2000) highlights the need to ensure environmental sustainability to efficiently poverty and support sustainable development. Many linkages can also be made between the environment and the Millennium Development goals. Furthermore the developing countries and industrialized nations have ratified various multilateral environmental agreements in order to save the environment. This calls for global partnership to improve research for the necessary technical information for the good of local, national and international community. This helps in capacity building that helps to mobilize resources for sustainable programs. It will help to fight common problems of hunger, poverty, diseases that hinder growth of most economies. There is however seemingly no tremendous changes in reducing poverty levels in developing countries due lack of good policies to reduce income disparities between the poor and the rich. This therefore poses a threat to the environment because of failure to route out poverty.

Good governance in across the world is an important ingredient for environmental management and sustainable development. In most countries, there lacks stringent measures to root out corruption tendencies, investment guidelines, affirmative action for women empowerment and empowered democratic institutions that are necessary for sustainable development. It will tend to inculcate the sense of nationalism and people's love for their countries that will create hospitable communities that will readily fit within the global fittings. They create an enabling environment for investment and create democratic principles in society. The ways by which people in the rest of the world live impacts people's lifestyles in particular country due to globalization. There is still need for international cooperation in areas of finance and technology to help economies that are not doing very well. Poor economies have continued to face enormous challenges like debt burden and poor terms of trade. Poor standard of living of the nationals in these countries is the order of the day. The gap between the very poor and the very rich keeps widening in such countries.

Proper planning is necessary for well designed programs, that is, local and community programs for sustainable development. These are meant to empower people living in poverty, and enable them access productive resources and public services. For example land, water, education and health, employment opportunities and credit are important for sustainable development. Basic education is however necessary to equip people with skills and knowledge to use the resources. A learned population turns challenges into opportunities. It is able to create resources for development.

Involving women in planning and policy development is essential for sustainable development. This involvement should be both at the planning and implementation levels. This will help to elevate a woman who mobilizes resources in our communities. It will help to eliminate gender violence that is a vice against development. It will also eliminate all forms of discrimination in regard to resource accessibility, employment, education and health. Women are in better position to bring about sustainable development because of family responsibilities they hold in most of the communities.

At school, we have tried to incorporate caring for the environment as part of what we do. We use the school compound to show how students should care for the environment. There are trees planted to provide the shed. Of recent we are introducing the fruit trees so that they will provide fruits that provide food security for a healthy population. At my home I and my wife tend to realize that when some vegetables are planted around the house, it will be beneficial to the family. We are saving some little money out of vegetables we have to produce around the house. When I travel to the village I educate my parents to plant their own trees for fuel and have efficiently utilized this resource. They have adopted technologies of producing fruits for their home consumption. This makes them save some money that is used to buy other necessities.

Chapter Five.

5.0 Recommendations.

There should be an effort by government and community based organizations to work with the community to foster sustainable livelihoods and protect biodiversity. Governments should learn from Central America and Mexico where unique landscapes have been conserved by putting the poor, rural communities in charge of managing local natural resources. This is because the local communities are better stewards of their local natural resources.

Institutions should work with community led water committees to protect their water sources through watershed management. People should easily access the knowledge of how resources should be used sustainably for the health of the people and for the good of the ecosystem. Interference of the water system affects both the life of human being, animals and climate change. Failure to preserve the water system generally affects the ecosystem.

Forest Conservation needs a lot of commitment by all players. Forests can be preserved through reforestation, installation of fuel efficient stoves, having protected areas management plans, and having workable policies to protect the environment.

The community based organizations should work with their partners and local communities to foster stewardship of the local forests. This should be done through forest management plans, reforestation of degraded forests, agro forestry, fuel efficient burning woods and using forest guards to patrol and protect forests.

Sustainable livelihood alternatives should be provided. Lack of alternatives is the major reason why the rural poor degrade natural resources. It is prudent to provide non timber forest products and enterprise and also promote sustainable agriculture. Masses should be educated on the importance of income generating activities. These include the rural poor and semi urban who heavily relies on the environment for survival. These projects allow the people to save and invest would enable them change their lifestyles. Emphasis on policy to enhance the industrial productivity should involve the transfer of technological sound technologies.

Sustainable agriculture should be improved. Demand for agricultural land poses one of the greatest threats to forest resources. Because of traditional clearing and burning practices, it makes land lose the necessary nutrients. This is because farmers are continuously looking for new fertile lands for agriculture. The solution to this problem is to find alternative ways of survival other than directly depending on the environment.

Non- Timber Forest Products should be provided. Provision of non-timber products to the rural poor is very important to preserve the ecosystem. Instead of competing with forests for land use, economic activities such as bee keeping, seed collection, sustainable rubber harvesting and tree resin collection take place within the forest cover. These activities are income generating while at the same time conserving the environment. This therefore leads us to an environmental management for a sustainable development.

Communities can come together to form Community Enterprises is important for a common identity. There should be community led management of natural resources. For example this has been true among the women groups of Guatemala binding together to grow and sell vegetables. Community efforts act as a ground for more sophiscated cooperative models. Togetherness leads to multiple ideas and owning of all decisions that makes Implementation of policy easier. Sharing of ideas makes individuals realize the importance of proper allocation of resources and this leads to sustainable development. Skills are imparted to the beneficiaries and check points are created within the society and this is more effective than the formal policies from the central government.

Institutions should provide community outreach and special training programs in farming practices, crop rotation, food production, livestock rearing, and vocational skills. These programs empower local farmers and enable them to generate sustainable incomes. The government and relevant organizations should provide community outreach and trainings in farming, crop rotation, livestock rearing, food production, and vocational skills are also a guarantee of food security. This encourages proper management of resources such as use of more efficient use of fuel and adoption of new technologies.

Creating advocacy campaigns and increase community participation creates people's passion in the environment. This increases their participation in sustainable utilization of natural resources, participation in the proper sanitation practices, and control of malaria and water borne diseases. These good practices, lead to improved lifestyles and hence sustainable development. Young people should be made to understand climate change and involve them in environmental conservation activities. This would involve equipping the youth with resources and knowledge through various youth programs. This can also be addressed in schools when environmental issues are clearly integrated in the school curriculum. In Uganda environmental issues are not clearly stipulated on the school curriculum. These issues are just taken as secondary. People are engaged in environment matters at an advanced age. This makes comprehension of the same difficult and unsustainable.

There are some important values that governments have to inculcate in young people. These include patriotism and love for the environment among the youth. By doing so, it becomes easy for the environmentalists to implement the environmental policy. It will also enhance environment awareness and management skills within the population.

Community bye laws, government policies and programs is essential for sustainable development. The population at the grass root is directly in touch with most of the natural resources which makes them giant stakeholders in matters of environment policies. Without them laws regarding environment will be abused. It is important for environmental institutions to adopt sustainability in resource management and create a shared vision and explain clearly the importance of environmental sustainability to the population. This is likely to have a far reaching effect on the environment.

Research on how to conserve the resources, to alleviate food shortages and implement sustainable farming practices should be upheld. These should reflect environmentally sound principles. There will be improved standards of living and reduced danger on the environment. The use of fossils has a big impact on the environment. There is therefore need to change the sources of energy from fossil fuels to renewable energy sources to avoid huge environmental impacts. For example Thailand has moved way from fossil fuels which used to account for the 90% of the electricity generated in the country. Gheewala (2011) asserts that this change to hydro power is particularly suitable for Thailand, and it is being applied at several locations. This however needs a lot of commitment on the part of respective governments and the entire international community. The type of technology is good for countries like East African countries where Hydro power potential is high.

Introduction of the appropriate local technologies is necessary. Approaches to local communities such as sustainable agriculture, fuel efficient stoves, organic demonstration gardens, water purification systems are important for environmental management for a sustainable development. Grass root communities should given a priority to adopt these technologies since they are directly in touch with the environment. It is vital to conduct qualitative and quantitative research, baseline studies and impact studies of community-based projects. These projects impact a lot on the environment as well as the welfare of the people.

Promoting integrated land management and water use plans based on sustainable use of renewable resources. These plans provide governments, local authorities and community's capacity to monitor and manage quantity and quality of land and water resources.

Community capacity building through training especially in the areas of technical expertise should be done. There will be capacity building in terms of life skills, nutrition, youth development, and income generating projects. It is reported that a common shortcoming in the environmental and other scientific fields is assuming that the public understands the usefulness, relevance, and applications of their work. It is important for the relevant institutions to avail timely information to the community. It is therefore necessary to develop a clear outreach strategy to enhance awareness.

Workshops, group activities, and stress relief activities that reduce community conflicts should be given a lot of attention. These workshops should involve the community, students and teachers, decision makers and researchers at all levels from the national to the local level. This requires the support of the civil society and politicians. This will multiply the beneficial effects on the environment, health and society.

Public awareness is important in this era of globalization. It is therefore important to develop radio programs, talk shows, advertising, and public relation programs that promote health, HIV/AIDS, and community development issues. A healthy population will ensure increased productivity that result into an improved standard of living. Once health has been promoted, a lot funds are saved that would go to medical health care. All this will lead to development that is sustainable. Implementation of national, international programs will help the affected and the infected to get relief from the pandemic and resort to development. The efforts of the international community should not be frustrated at the implementation level. Follow up of the Global fund money is very necessary since some public servants are corrupt and would always want to encroach on the money meant for the disadvantaged.

At the international level, the US secretary of state Hillary Clinton has announced a renewed commitment by the US president to end the AIDS epidemic, media reports have said. It is a commitment by the US government by embarking on intensive research. She calls upon partnering countries to increase commitment in terms of resources. Uganda is on this program but it not doing well in implementing AIDS programs and achieving the maximum healthcare of the population. For example, more than 40% of Ugandans who are in need of ARVs cannot access them and 20% of the mothers still pass on HIV to their children. There is need of all development partners to step up their efforts towards combating HIV. HIV has greatly affected development in developing countries, Uganda inclusive.

It is very important to develop Information and Communications technology to allow the rural poor to access information. NEMA has been using internet to communicate with local and global audience about environmental issues but it has been facing a lot of challenges for example lack of facilities, power shortages low internet band width and the laxity of the population. Informed people are better equipped to participate in looking for solutions to problems that affect them. They are more likely to play a meaningful role in environmental decision making and to take advantage of the opportunities for environmental justice.

Involving the grass root people in the environmental planning is very important. A bottom up planning is preferred to avoid implementation difficulties. Selin. S. and Chavez. (1995) explains that those which are more traditional and stick to hierarchical decision making are having difficulty dealing with the demand for lateral decision making that supports effective participation. This therefore calls environmental institutions to involve all stake holders in environmental planning. The community knows the problems affecting them better. It should therefore be used in planning and implementation to its maximum capacity. The local population is in position to deal with challenges such as bush burning, poaching and deciding on how to move away from forest life for a competitive life system like commerce, education and commercial agriculture.

Environmental issues should be properly planned for. Planning should include the implementation and monitoring strategies. Environmental monitoring should be done in relation to the environment set objectives. Environmental assessment is helpful in planning environment integration and decision making. This will promote environmental management and sustainable development. This will promote efficient use of sources of energy so that they are used.

Serious implementation of the law is very crucial for instance the forest law. This should include international trade in illegal forest and animal products. It is more practical with the involvement of the international community in collaboration with the local authorities. Institutional capacity building can be built to conserve the environment is stronger when all players are involved to curb the related vices. These measures empower all the stakeholders to do what is within their means to achieve sustainable development.

All means possible to achieve sustainable harvesting of timber and to facilitate provision of financial resources and development of environmentally sound technologies and other environmentally friendly practices.

Regional and international cooperation and partnerships are necessary to facilitate trade, natural resource management, capacity building and technology transfer meant for natural resource preservation.

Capacity building in research, science and technology is needed for sustainable development. A lot of follow up and funding is required to provide information, skills, and knowledge. This will bring about sustainable development through eradication of poverty, hunger, diseases and environmental degradation. In Uganda some children do not attend school because of lack of food at home despite free education. A hungry person cannot concentrate in class.

Chapter six.

6.0 Conclusion.

For sustainable development to occur there must be effective management of the environment. Sustainable management of natural resources is very important for any country's modern economic development. Policy makers should be so careful when dealing with natural resources. Some of the natural resources are non-renewable that they can be depleted any time. Proper management of natural resources is essential for sustainable development. It entails using the proceeds of these resources to spur core economic sectors like infrastructure, industry, such that the economy becomes a self integrated and competing. Effective management of natural resources is the key to meet the basic requirements of the rural poor.

The community is an important entity in managing of the natural resources. Their level of participation and the quality of information provided is important for the use and sustainability of these resources. Basic training is therefore necessary to equip them with skills and to expose them to new ideas and approaches.

Fundamental changes such as promotion of sustainable consumption patterns and production methods are necessary for countries to achieve global sustainable development. There should be efficiency and sustainability in the use of resources and production processes. This helps in the reduction of resource depletion, pollution and waste.

There is need for man to use the natural resources in a sustainable way so that the future generations are not suffocated. Improper use of the natural resources leads to natural disasters, poverty, hunger and diseases. Economic welfare of the people is important for nations to attain environmental management and sustainable development.

Sustainable use of forest resources is essential towards achieving sustainable development. Renewable energy sources should be adopted. This would help to ease the work of poverty eradication, reduce natural resource degradation and improve the food security. It will also achieve health standards and improvement of the general welfare. The achievement of sustainable natural resource management is essential for sustainable development.

Human activities have had an increasing impact on the ecosystem. It is the natural environment that provides the life support for man. It requires proper management of the natural environment for it to provide man with the best services he deserves. Man taps the best from a well maintained ecosystem .To reverse the current trend of natural resource degradation, it is necessary to implement strategies that are designed by the relevant organs at to protect the ecosystems. It is important to develop a more practical system that can lead to sustainable development and poverty reduction.

There is need for the government especially those that depend on agriculture, to provide great support to the agriculture sector. This can be in terms of allocating budget funds for rural infrastructure, farm diversification, veterinary, sanitary and phytosanitary laboratories and equipment in order to raise agricultural productivity. This will improve the incomes of the people such that they move away from dependence on fragile areas of forests and wetlands. Warren (2013), shows that poor budgeting leads to poor rural infrastructure and this greatly affects agricultural trade, farm diversification and ultimately poverty.

Acronyms

AIDS   Acquired Immune Deficiency Syndrome.

EAC   East African Community.

CO_2 Carbon dioxide.

NEMA NATIONAL Environment Management Authority.

NGO   Non Governmental Organization.

PES   Payment for Ecosystem Services.

TASO The AIDS Support Organization.

LDC.   Low Carbon Development.

References.

Agatha (2012). Forest encroachers at risk. (Daily Monitor 25th Oct 2012). Kampala.

Ariho (2013). Tree planting. (Daily Monitor 11th Jan 2013). Kampala.

Atuheire (2012). Banana fibre bags better packaging option. (New Vision 4th Oct. 2012). Kampala.

Bian, Bo, Cheng, Xiao- Juano; Li, Lei.(2011). Investigations of the urban water quality using simulated rain fall in a medium size city of China. *Environment monitoring and Assessment* 183. No. 1-4, 217-229.

Dyllick,T. and Hockerts, K.(2002). Beyond the business case for corporate sustainability. *Business Strategy and the Environment,* 11(2): 130-141.

Daly, H.E.(1991). Steady-State Economics(2nd ed.) Washington, D.C: Island Press.

Dora Byamukama (2013). Health, older persons are a resource to family, economy. (New Vision 14th Oct 2012).

Gastone, N (2013). *We need more forests Mabira Inclusive*. Daily Monitor of 16th Jan 2013). Kampala.

Goote Rogers.(2011). Equitable regulation of private forests. *Small scale factory* 10, no.4 , 457-472.

Gheewala Shabbir, H. (2011). Life cycle assessment of mini-hydro power plants in Thailand. The international journal of life cycle Assessment 16, no.9(2011). 849-858.

Grasso, Marco.(2011). The role of justice in the North-South conflict in climate change: *the case of negotiations on the Adaptation Fund. International Environment agreements: Politics, Law, and Economics* 11 no.4 , 361-377.

J. Prof. Nurs. (1999). Environmental management. *Principles of quantum theory,* 15(4): 209-213

Koont, Sinan (2011). *Sustainable Urban Agriculture.* Florida: University Press of Florida.

Lwamafa (2012). Forest encroachers at risk. (Daily Monitor 25th Oct 2012). Kampala.

Namutebi (2012). Fishing nets queried. (Daily Monitor 9th July 2012). Kampala.

NEMA Report (1998). Uganda

NEMA Report (2004). Uganda.

Millennium Promise, (2011). Annual, Report on Millennium Villages Project.

Pennington, David W, Versmann, Andreas. (2011). Supporting environmentally sound decisions for waste managent wit LCT and LCA. *The international Journal of Life Cycle Assessmnet* 16, no. 9(2011). 937-939.

Richard Kimbowa (2013). Shrinking forest. (New Vision 15th Jan 2013). Kampala.

Saneh, E.S. (2011). Introduction of a recycling system for sustainable municipal solid waste management: A case study of greater Banjul area of the Gambia. *Development and sustainability,* 6, 1065-1080.

Selin. S., and Chavez. D., 1995, Developing a Collaborative Model for Environmental Planning and Management, *Environmental Management,* Vol.19, pp. 189-195.

Steward, Alisha.(2011). Terrestrial Invertebrates of dry river beds are not simply subsets of riparian assemblages. Aquatic sciences,4, 551-556.

Umrani etal (2010). *Sustainable Agriculture.* London: Oxford Book Co.

Sunday Vision (23rd October 2011).

Smith, Charles; Rees,Gareth.(1998). Economic Development.(2nd ed.). Basingstoke: Macmillan.

Warren (2012). Address Agricultural Inequity. (New Vision 4th Oct 20102). Kampala.

Will Allen.(2007). *Learning for sustainability: Sustainable Development.*

http://www.nemaug.org/

http://wikipedia.org.wiki/sustainable -*sustainable devlopment.*